YOUR KNOWLEDGE HAS

- We will publish your bachelor's and master's thesis, essays and papers

- Your own eBook and book - sold worldwide in all relevant shops

- Earn money with each sale

Upload your text at www.GRIN.com and publish for free

Bibliographic information published by the German National Library:

The German National Library lists this publication in the National Bibliography; detailed bibliographic data are available on the Internet at http://dnb.dnb.de .

Imprint:

Copyright © 2016 GRIN Verlag, Open Publishing GmbH
Print and binding: Books on Demand GmbH, Norderstedt Germany
ISBN: 9783668261716

This book at GRIN:

http://www.grin.com/en/e-book/322550/is-prior-knowledge-necessary-for-undergra-duate-computing-courses-a-study

Yeeshtdevisingh Hosanee

Is prior knowledge necessary for undergraduate computing courses? A study of courses offered by Mauritian universities

GRIN Publishing

GRIN - Your knowledge has value

Since its foundation in 1998, GRIN has specialized in publishing academic texts by students, college teachers and other academics as e-book and printed book. The website www.grin.com is an ideal platform for presenting term papers, final papers, scientific essays, dissertations and specialist books.

Visit us on the internet:

http://www.grin.com/

http://www.facebook.com/grincom

http://www.twitter.com/grin_com

No prior computing knowledge is required from A-level holders in most Mauritians universities undergraduate computing courses

Yeeshtdevisingh Hosanee

Abstract

Prior computing knowledge is not a pre-requisite for enrolling in many computing undergraduate courses at many universities. It is said that the difficulty of learning computer programming lies only with the logic thinking of the student, not because they did not have prior computing knowledge. Universities all around the world are putting tremendous effort to encourage and support students to acquire basic computing skills and computer programming skills. Therefore in this paper, an analysis of all undergraduate computing courses offered in 2015 by two main Mauritian universities, the University of Technology (UTM) and University of Mauritius (UOM) is carried out. This analysis includes two phases: the first one allows us to identify all computing courses which do not require prior computing knowledge at A-Level to enroll in these courses. The second phase will help us to identify the computing courses which are teaching computer programming. From the two analysis we will be able to understand the number of computing courses not requiring computing at A level but will give non -computing A-level students the chance to learn computer programming at tertiary level.

Keywords:
Computing, Information and communication technologies (ICT), Information Technology (IT), computer programming.

1. Introduction

The world is turning into a digital world and the need to have computer literate nations is becoming important [1]. Jodie Lopez, Champion Schools Coordinator at Pearson said that we are used to drawing on papers. But now the world is changing, the art will be on computers. Computer graphics, graphics design and so on. A new world which should be considered [2].Many countries around the world are working towards a digital society [3, 4, 5].For developing countries [6, 7], the implementation of a digital culture is more challenging [8, 9]compared to its implementation in developed countries. Mauritius among many of these developing countries[10] is also putting much effort to turn the island into a cyber island [11].Different strategies and different effort are being done to work towards it. For instance, in August 2015, the prime minister of Mauritius launched "the Mauritius Vision 2030" [12]. It is a committee which has main task to explore different strategies to boost the economy of the country. The digital economy is one of its primary concerns. Other initiatives such as the pilot project known as "Hsc professional" [13], the caravan project [14] and the ICT in the form1-3 syllabus [15] will definitely contribute to the ICT development of the country [16].

To be able to achieve this change successfully, we need to alter the mindset of the society. The existing mindset is to hand-write on papers. The new vision is to allow everybody to use Information communication and technology (ICT) devices to write and share data [17]. People need to adapt themselves to a world where they need to communicate effectively with the different ICT devices such as computers, mobile phones, tablets and laptops.Besides knowing how to use the software in these different devices, we also need to teach people how to build these software even though they do not intent to have a career in the IT[18]. Teaching students to build software consists of teaching them of the different computer programming skills which exist today. However, the complexity of computer programming often makes students run away from computing classes[19, 20].Therefore, we need to teach students whatever we need in our new industry[21, 22]. Many universities and secondary schools are currently in the process of making computing classes important in their curriculum to meet the job market requirements[23]. Therefore, in this paper we highlight the contribution of two main universities in Mauritius to the ICT sector. In 2015, both the University of Mauritius and University of Technology Mauritius allow non-computing A-level holders to enroll to computing courses provided they have the minimum pass mark required in their non-computing subjects.In addition to encourage non-computing A-level students to enroll in IT courses, these universities are also making effort to teach computer programming to students [24, 25]. Therefore, two analyses were carried out. The first analysis is on the effort that these two tertiary institutions are putting forward to encourage maximum students to learn Computing. The second analysis is on the effort making by these institutions to teach computer programming to students.

2.   Background study

Having one teacher for each student was seen to be costly for many countries[26]. Computers have allowed students to learn more beyond a classroom. The internet helps students to widen their knowledge and their different academic expertise [26]. Since 2004, all schools in Bavaria (one of the federal states of Germany), made computer science compulsory in their secondary schools to encourage students to learn computing [5]. Object-oriented programming is made compulsory in these schools[5].Word processors, spreadsheets, paint programs are taught not only like simple everyday tools, but as examples of computer programming too" [4]. In Nigeria [27], students who do not have access to internet and computers are most likely to get further behind their peers who do have these facilities. Examinations in Nigeria are carried out on computers in universities[27].Therefore, Nigerian undergraduatestudents need to have ICT skills and knowledge [28, 27].This strategy allows most of Nigerians postgraduate's students not to have any issues with computer skills[29]. On the other hand, Pakistan is perceived to be in a state of infancy regarding technologies and thus, there exists a great hindrance in transforming knowledge into new technologies [30].

Computer literacy is important [31, 32, 33] for many of us whether we are thinking to have a career in IT or any other field. For instance, even non-computing teachers[18] need to understand how a software works because they will need to use software to teach in their respective class. Linguistic teachers used linguistic software tools to teach their particular language. The teacher is expected to understand how these tools work.Programming skills are also seen useful for many scientists who does not have any prior background of computing [34]. As it can be seen, for sure, computer literacy brings many benefits to the job market[35].Some universities are making computer literacy a requirement for graduation[36, 37]. Some medical universities emphasise on making their medical students acquire some computing skills as well[38]. Australian universities[39] and many other universities[40, 41] around the world are actively conducting research and experiments to support computer programming students.Unesco is also encouraging and helping African countries to teach computing and computer programming[42].Unesco made a guide[42] known as the "unesco guide to measure ict in edu" which allows teachers to promote computing classes in a standard way. This guide was purposely meant to be used by African countries to boost their economy. Mauritius being an African countries, is also making effort to promote ICT in the country[43].

It is true that prior computing knowledge is not required to enroll in many computing courses[44]. However,the lack of computing is not seen to be a big problem. But the lack of logic thinking and problem solving skills is a major concern[44] for many universities.Many novice computer programming tools are being developed to support students to learn computer programming[45, 24]. Such tools include Alice, blueJ, Greenfoot, dragon-drop and many others[45, 24].

3.   Methodology

The methodology of this research is a quantitative analysis of all the undergraduate computing courses offered at both UOM and UTM in January 2015. The methodology consists of two parts. The first part is to identify the pre-requisite A-level subjects for undergraduate computing courses at these two tertiary institution and second part is to identify the undergraduate courses which are teaching computer programming to students. This analysis is being conducted by collecting the different undergraduate course structure documents which are available on each of these universities' website. Based on these documents, the pre-requisite A-level subjects and the course consisting of at least a computer programming module are identified. The data collected are tabulated in tables. In this paper, you will find all these tables in the section results. Pie charts and mathematical subsets are used to represent these data quantitatively.

4.   Results

4.1. Pre-requisite A-Level subject:

There exist two main universities in Mauritius. University of Technology Mauritius(UTM) and University of Mauritius(UOM). They offer several undergraduate computing courses. The pre-requisite A-Level subjects for a computing course in most of their undergraduate courses include "mathematics and science", "Mathematics only", "Computing", "Science or Computing" and "any 2-A level subjects".

Hence, the following table shows the computing courses offered in 2015 by these two universities and the A-level pre-requisite subjects needed to enroll in this particular computing course. The total number of courses in the table is fifteen. Among the fifteen computing courses, seven of them are UTM computing courses and the remaining eight computing courses are from UOM. The value "Yes" in the table indicates that the particular course require the respective A-level subjects.. For each undergraduate course, an acronym is assigned in the table so that the course can easily be referred in this paper.

For the second row of the table, an example is being given to understand how to read the table. The university of Technology (UTM) is offering Bsc (Hons) Business information Systems. Any 2-A level subjects can be acceptable as an entry for this course (i.e the "Yes" value is in the last column). The same logic applies to the remaining rows in the table.

Table 1 showing the subjects required at A-LEVEL for the 15 courses which have at least 1 IT module in its entire course.

University	Acronym	Courses [56, 57]	mathematics and science	mathematics	computing	science or computing	mathematics or computing	Any 2-A level
UTM	A	BSc. (Hons) Business Information Systems						Yes
UTM	B	BSc (Hons.) Green Computing and communications	Yes					
UTM	C	BSc (Hons.) Software Engineering					Yes	
UTM	D	BSC (Hons) Web Technologies						Yes
UTM	E	BSc (Hons) computer science with network security	Yes		Yes			
UTM	F	BSc (Hons) Accounting with Finance Information Systems						Yes
UTM	G	BSc (Hons) Mathematics		Yes				
UOM	H	BSc (Hons) Mathematics		Yes				
UOM	I	BSc (Hons) Mathematics with Computer Science		Yes				
UOM	J	BSc (Hons) Electronics	Yes					

		with Computer Science						
UOM	K	BSc (Hons) Information and Communication Technologies	Yes					
UOM	L	BSc (Hons) Software Engineering		Yes				
UOM	M	BSc (Hons) Information Systems						
UOM	N	BSc (Hons) Computer Science		Yes		Yes		
UOM	O	BSc (Hons) Applied Computing					Yes	

The data in the previous table is being represented graphically in the following pie chart for statistical analysis. Among the 15 (100%) computing courses, 27 % of the courses require "Mathematics and science" A-level subjects for its course entry. Another 27 % of the remaining computing courses, only Mathematics as A-Level subject is required. 6% of the courses have the option of either a computing A-level subject or a science A-level subject, but with compulsory Mathematics. 13 % have the options of choosing either computing or maths. 20 % of the courses allows A-level holders to enroll in their course with any A-level subjects providing the pass mark is accepted. Finally, only 7 % of the courses requires three subjects (computing, a science subject and mathematics). To conclude, computing at A-level is seen to be an optional for all the 93 % of undergraduate computing courses at these two institutions.

The following diagram represents the figures as described in the previous paragraph.

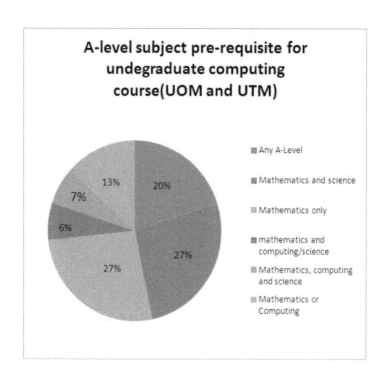

A-level subject pre-requisite for undegraduate computing course(UOM and UTM)

- Any A-Level
- Mathematics and science
- Mathematics only
- mathematics and computing/science
- Mathematics, computing and science
- Mathematics or Computing

The following table describes the previous pie chart numerically:

Table 2 showing the percentage for pre-requisite subjects category

Categories for pre-requisite of computing undergraduate course for both UTM and UOM	Number of courses per category	Percentage
Any A-Level	3	20
Mathematics and science	4	27
Mathematics only	4	27
mathematics and computing/science	1	6
Mathematics, computing and science	1	7
Mathematics or Computing	2	13

4.2. Computing courses consisting of at least one computing programming module:

Among all the 15 computing courses listed in table 1, some of them do include computer programming module in their course and some of them do not have computer programming module in their course. Therefore, in table 3, we have listed all courses with their respective IT module(programming and non-programming). For instance bsc(hons) in business Information Systems have Structured programming and Internet Programming which allows its students to learn computer programming. On the other hand, bsc in accounting with Finance information systems do not have computer programming module, but it teaches its students other computing skills. "ICT in organisations" is the module in which these students are able to learn these particular computing skills.

Table 3 computer programming/non-computer programming module per course

University	Acronym	Computing course [56,57]	Computer programming IT modules [56,57]	non-computer programming IT modules [56,57]
UTM	A	BSc. (Hons) Business Information Systems	Structured Programming , Internet Programming	
UTM	B	BSc (Hons.) Green Computing and communications	Object Oriented Software Development I, Object Oriented Software Development II	
UTM	C	BSc (Hons.) Software Engineering	Object Oriented Software Development I, Object Oriented Software Development II	
UTM	D	BSC (Hons) Web Technologies	Object-oriented	
UTM	E	BSc (Hons) computer science with network security	Object Oriented Software Development 1	
UTM	F	BSc (Hons) Accounting with Finance Information Systems		ICT in Organisations
UTM	G	BSc (Hons) Mathematics	Computer programming	
UOM	H	BSc (Hons) Mathematics	linear programming	Computer Applications in Mathematics
UOM	I	BSc (Hons) Mathematics with Computer Science	Computer Programming I	Introduction to IT
UOM	J	BSc (Hons) Electronics with Computer Science	Computer Programming	
UOM	K	BSc (Hons) Information and Communication	Computer Programming	

		Technologies		
UOM	L	BSc (Hons) Software Engineering	Software Programming, Object-Oriented Software Development	
UOM	M	BSc (Hons) Information Systems	Object-Oriented Programming	Communication and Business Skills for IT, Mathematics for Information Systems
UOM	N	BSc (Hons) Computer Science	Computer Programming,	Mathematics for Computer Science, Communication and Business Skills for IT
UOM	O	BSc (Hons) Applied Computing	Programming Principles and Algorithms	Mathematics for Computing, Communication and Business Skills for IT

The following diagram represents the data collected in a subset for ease of understanding:

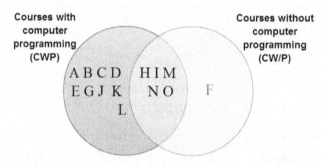

Courses with computer programming (CWP)

Courses without computer programming (CW/P)

A B C D H I M
E G J K N O   F
L

Mathematical notation for number of undergraduate courses having a computer programming module:
n(CWP)= 14

Among the 15 computing courses, 14 of these courses consists of at least one module teaching computer programming. Only one (Bsc Accounting with finance information systems (F)) of the fifteen does not contain a programming module.

4.2. Overall conclusion of the two analyses:

Among all the fourteen courses teaching computer programming, only one (E: Bsc computer science and network security(UTM)) of the courses, has as pre-requisite, computing at A-level. On a statistical point of view, on average 92 %(13/14) of computer programming degree courses does not require computing at A-Level.

5.   Conclusion

The need to have computer programming in schools' and universities' curriculum is being emphasized all around the world[17, 46, 23]. Much effort are being carried out globally [47, 48, 49]. Computing courses given to non-computing students will definitely help them in their career[50]. Research shows that computing students are found to be more open-minded than non-computing students [51].

If we want Mauritius to become a cyber island we should encourage and motivate[52] people to acquire computing skills as a survey doneby the central statistic office(CSO) in 2016 confirmed that 62.9% of the surveyed persons were seen not having any knowledge in IT[53].

Therefore, the two univerisites in Mauritius are encouraging non-computing A-level holders to learn advanced computer skills. Students enrolling for most of computing undergraduate courses in Mauritius do not require prior computing knowledge[44]. This ultimately allows many of non-computing students to have the opportunity to learn computer programming and acquire more advanced computer skills at tertiary level. This is one of the many strategies the two Mauritian Universities are working towards computer literacy. There exists many other strategies as well. In future Mauritianuniversities shall make computer literacy a graduation requirements for non-IT students as computational thinking is seen to be for everyone[54] and can empower themselves[55].

Aknowledgement

I am grateful to both the University of Mauritius(UOM) and University of Technology Mauritius(UTM) for their available course structure documents on their respective website. Without these documents, it would have been difficult to perform this analysis.

References

[1]   D. P. Karrberg and D. J. Liebenau, "New Business Models in the Digital Economy Mobile service platforms and the apps economy," 2013.

[2]   J. Gurney, "telegraph," 2013. [Online]. Available: http://www.telegraph.co.uk/education/educationopinion/10436444/Digital-literacy-as-important-as-reading-and-writing.html. [Accessed 10 March 2015].

[3]   city&guilds, "Leading employers to shape the education and skills agenda," 2014.

[4]   kiss, "Computer science education in Germany," Proceedings of the 7th International Conference on Applied Informatics, vol. vol 2, p. 45–54, 2007.

[5]   A. Mühling, P. Hubwieser and T. Brinda, "Exploring Teachers' Attitudes Towards Object Oriented," 2010.

[6]   P. Sy, "public sphere project," [Online]. Available: http://www.publicsphereproject.org/node/388. [Accessed 30 03 2016].

[7]   A. Kumar, P. Reddy, A. Tewari, R. Agrawal and M. Kam, "Improving Literacy in Developing Countries Using Speech Recognition-Supported Games on Mobile Devices," ACM 978-1-4503-1015-4/12/05, 2012.

[8]   S. &. B. J. Kurbanoglu, "Information Literacy: Moving Toward Sustainability: Third European," 2015.

[9]   J. O. Oroma, H. Wanga and F. Ngumbuke, "Challenges of teaching and learning computer

programming in developing countries," in Proceedings of INTED2012 Conference:5th-7th March 2012, Valencia, Spain., 2012.

[10] WESP, "Statistical Annex," 2012.

[11] ict_authority, "The ICT sector in Mauritius," https://www.icta.mu/documents/publications/ictview.pdf, 2004.

[12] CIM, "CIM global business," 2015. [Online]. Available: https://www.cimglobalbusiness.com/news-official-launch-of-the-mauritius-vision-2030-.html. [Accessed 12 11 2015].

[13] LeMatinal, "Le HSC Professional Qualification sera introduit en 2015," 2013. [Online]. Available: http://www.orange.mu/kinews/dossiers/societe/352267/le-hsc-professional-qualification-sera-introduit-en-2015.html. [Accessed 04 04 2016].

[14] P. Teeloku, "e-Government Initiatives in Mauritius," Ministry of information and communication technology.

[15] MIE, "syllabus form I,II,III," Mauritius Institute of Education in Association with the Ministry of Education in association with the Ministry of Education & Human Resources, 2011.

[16] P. Leelachand, 2013. [Online]. Available: http://www.defimedia.info/news-sunday/nos-education/item/28941-hsc-professional-an-alternative-to-hsc-academic.html. [Accessed 10 March 2015].

[17] J. M. Ross and H. Zhang, "Structured Programmers Learning Object-Oriented Programming," 1997.

[18] R. Godwin-Jones, "The evolving roles of language teachers: trained coders, local researchers, global citizens," Special Issue on Teacher Education and CALL, p. 15, 2015.

[19] A. Ali and C. Shubra, "Efforts to Reverse the Trend of Enrollment Decline in computer science programs," vol. vol 7, no. Issues in Informing Science and Information Technology, 2010.

[20] L. Palmquist, "Exploring self-efficacy in end-user programming — a feminist approach," Exploring self-efficacy in end-user programming — a feminist approach, 2014.

[21] M. Kölling, "The problem of teaching object-oriented programming," 1999.

[22] D. Tapscott, "The Digital Economy ANNIVERSARY EDITION: Rethinking Promise and Peril in the age of networked intelligence," 2014.

[23] C. clark-Bishop and J. D. Kiper, "An Undergraduate Course in Object-Oriented Software Design," 1998.

[24] Y. &. P. S. Hosanee, "An enhanced software tool to aid novices in learning Object Oriented Programming (OOP)," in Computing, Communication and Security (ICCCS), 2015 International Conference , 2015.

[25] J. C. Adams, V. Bauer and S. Baichoo, "An Expanding Pipeline: Gender in Mauritius," ACM 1-58113-648-X/03/0002, 2003.

[26] K. Koedinger, "Cognitive Tutors: Technology Bringing Learning Science to the Classroom," 2006.

[27] O. &. N. B. Patrick, "COMPUTER LITERACY AMONG UNDERGRADUATE STUDENTS IN NIGERIA UNIVERSITIES," British Journal of Education, vol. 2, pp. pp.1-8, 2014.

[28] O. Eme, M. Emmanuel and O. Ernest, "Computer Studies and Its impact in Secondary Schools in Umuahia-North Local Government Area of Abia State, Nigeria," MECS:Modern Education and Computer Science, pp. pp.16-23, 2015.

[29] D. &. A. A. Abubakar, "INFLUENCE OF COMPUTER LITERACY ON POSTGRADUATES USE OF E-RESOURCES IN NIGERIAN UNIVERSITY LIBRARIES," 2015.

[30] M. Awan, "Comuter literacy for academic and national development: Role of Universities in Pakistan," http://cemca.org.in/ckfinder/userfiles/Awan_Muhammad_Daud__0225.pdf.

[31] K. Tyler, "The Problems in Computer Literacy Training," http://www.ccs.neu.edu/home/romulus/papers/mywr/report.htm, 1998.

[32] A. &. C. F. AHMAD, "Computer Literacy Program: A Study of Adult Student Perspectives," 2002.

[33] K. Wasiyo, "Increasing Computer Literacy in Africa," In African Technology Forum.

[34] D. Valle and A. Berdanier, "Computer Programming Skills for Environmental Sciences," http://sfrc.ufl.edu/facultysites/valle/programming_skills.pdf, 2012.

[35] L. &. M. D. Latzko, "smallbusiness," [Online]. Available:

http://smallbusiness.chron.com/advantages-being-computer-literate-workforce-27703.html. [Accessed 30 03 2016].

[36] R. Reinoehl and B. Mueller, "Computer Literacy in Human Services Education," 2008.

[37] C. e. a. Crawford, "Computer Literacy Defined and Implemented as University Graduation Requirement," in In Proceedings of Society for Information Technology & Teacher Education International Conference, 2003.

[38] K. Gibson and M. Silverberg, "A two-year experience teaching computer literacy to first-year medical students using skill-based cohorts," 2000.

[39] M. d. Raadt, R. Watson and M. Toleman, "Introductory Programming Languages at Australian Universities at the Beginning of the Twenty First Century," 2003.

[40] A. Kak, "Teaching Programming," https://engineering.purdue.edu/kak/TeachingProgramming.pdf, 2008.

[41] J. WELSH, "The University of Chicago," 2016. [Online]. Available: https://masters.cs.uchicago.edu/page/no-computer-science-background. [Accessed 03 04 2016].

[42] unesco, "GUIDE TO MEASURING INFORMATION AND COMMUNICATION TECHNOLOGIES (ICT) IN EDUCATION," http://unesdoc.unesco.org/images/0018/001865/186547e.pdf, 2009.

[43] V. Bhoyroo, "ICT in Mauritius," http://euroafrica-ict.org/wp-content/plugins/alcyonis-event-agenda//files/ICT_in_Mauritius_-_e-learning_vision_and_governance.pdf, 2015.

[44] I. Miliszewska and G. Tan, "Befriending Computer Programming: A Proposed Approach to teaching introductory programming," 2007.

[45] S. SILESSI, H. VAROL, O. KOLAWOLE, D. KEY and B. HOUCK, "Dragon Drop Pictorial Programming," 2013.

[46] computing-at-school, "Computer Science as a school subject Seizing the opportunity," 2012. [Online]. Available: http://www.computingatschool.org.uk/data/uploads/Case%20for%20Computing.pdf. [Accessed 10 March 2015].

[47] C. Hockings, S. Cooke, H. Yamashita, S. McGinty and M. Bowl, "Switched off? A study of disengagement among computing students at two universities," Research Papers in Education Special Issue on Higher Education, 2008.

[48] M. J. Druzdzel, "TECHNOLOGY USE IN COMPUTER PROGRAMMING COURSES Technology in Teaching, Pittsburgh, Pennsylvania, March 29, 1996," 1996.

[49] S. M. Taheri, M. Sasaki, J. O. Chu and H. T. Ngetha, "A Study of Teaching Problem Solving and Programming to Children by Introducing a New Programming Language," The International Journal of E-Learning and Educational Technologies in the Digital Media (IJEETDM) 2(1), pp. 31-36, 2016.

[50] W. L. X. &. L. W. Chen, "Teaching Computer Programming to Non-computer Science Students," in In The Asian Conference on Education Official Conference Proceedings , 2011.

[51] P. Alexander, V. Pieterse and H. and Lotriet, "A COMPARISON OF COMPUTING AND NON-COMPUTING STUDENTS' PERSONALITIES BASED ON THE FIVE-FACTOR MODEL," in ECIS 2011 Proceedings, 2011.

[52] S. &. B. J. Kurbanoglu, "Information Literacy: Moving Toward Sustainability: Third European.," 2015. [Online]. Available: http://smallbusiness.chron.com/advantages-being-computer-literate-workforce-27703.html. [Accessed 01 04 2016].

[53] C. Chan-Meetoo, "ICT, Society and Poverty:The Vision of Mauritius as a Cyber island from a Development Perspective:," 2007.

[54] J. M. Wing, "Computational Thinking," COMMUNICATIONS OF THE ACM , vol. 49, no. 3, 2006.

[55] A. Kelly, "Technology can empower children in developing countries - if it's done right," 2013. [Online]. Available: http://www.theguardian.com/sustainable-business/technology-empower-children-developing-countries . [Accessed 30 03 2016].

[56] UTM, 2015. [Online]. Available: http://www.utm.ac.mu/index.php/en/features/undergraduate-

programmes/132-undergraduate-programmes-site. [Accessed 10 March 2015].

[57] UOM, 2015. [Online]. Available: http://www.uom.ac.mu/foe/index.php/cse-programmes. [Accessed 10 March 2015].

YOUR KNOWLEDGE HAS VALUE